MICHIGAN STATE
SPARTANS

BY J CHRIS ROSELIUS

Published by ABDO Publishing Company, PO Box 298166, Minneapolis, MN 55439. Copyright © 2012 by Abdo Consulting Group, Inc. International copyrights reserved in all countries. No part of this book may be reproduced in any form without written permission from the publisher. SportsZone™ is a trademark and logo of ABDO Publishing Company.

Printed in the United States of America,
North Mankato, Minnesota
102011
012012

Editor: Chrös McDougall
Copy Editor: Bo Smolka
Design and production: Craig Hinton

Photo Credits: James Drake/Sports Illustrated/Getty Images, cover, 7; David J. Phillip/AP Images, 1; Heinz Kluetmeier/Sports Illustrated/Getty Images, 4, 43 (top right); Rich Clarkson/Sports Illustrated/Getty Images, 9; Rich Clarkson/Time & Life Pictures/Getty Images, 10; David R. Frazier Photolibrary, Inc./Alamy, 12; AP Images, 15, 23, 42 (top); MCP/AP Images, 18, 43 (top left); RMK/AP Images, 20; Jonathan Daniel/Allsport/Getty Images, 25; Dave Martin/AP Images, 26, 31; Ryan McKee/NCAA Photos/AP Images, 28, 37, 42 (bottom); Brian Gadbery/NCAA Photos/AP Images, 33, 43 (bottom left); Al Goldis/AP Images, 34, 44; Eric Gay/AP Images, 39; John Raoux/AP Images, 40, 43 (bottom right)

Design elements: Matthew Brown/iStockphoto

Library of Congress Cataloging-in-Publication Data
Roselius, J Chris.
  Michigan State Spartans / by J. Chris Roselius.
    p. cm. -- (Inside college basketball)
  Includes index.
  ISBN 978-1-61783-285-7
1. Michigan State University--Basketball--History--Juvenile literature. 2. Michigan State Spartans (Basketball team)--History--Juvenile literature. I. Title.
  GV885.43.M53R67 2012
  796.323'630977427--dc23
  [B]
                          2011040002

TABLE OF CONTENTS

1 TWO YEARS OF MAGIC..............5

2 BABY STEPS..................13

3 THE HEATHCOTE ERA................21

4 CHAMPIONS AGAIN....................29

5 STAYING ELITE..........................35

TIMELINE 42

QUICK STATS 44

QUOTES & ANECDOTES 45

GLOSSARY 46

INDEX 48

ABOUT THE AUTHOR 48

Michigan State's Earvin "Magic" Johnson dribbles up the court during a 1978 game against Kentucky.

TWO YEARS OF MAGIC

TOM IZZO BECAME HEAD COACH OF THE MICHIGAN STATE SPARTANS IN 1995. THROUGH 2011, HE HAS LED THE SPARTANS TO SIX FINAL FOURS. BUT FOR MANY, THE TEAM'S MOST MEMORABLE MOMENTS OCCURRED FROM 1977 TO 1979. THAT IS WHEN A GAME-CHANGING PLAYER NAMED EARVIN "MAGIC" JOHNSON PLAYED FOR THE SPARTANS.

Johnson grew up only miles away from the Michigan State campus, which is located in East Lansing. The season before Johnson arrived at Michigan State, the Spartans finished with a 12–15 record. But when Johnson, a point guard, arrived for the 1977–78 season, it was easy to see he was a special talent. In addition to tremendous ability, Johnson stood 6 feet, 9 inches tall. That is several inches taller than the typical point guard.

"When he came in it became very obvious, along with Jay Vincent, it was obvious that now we were championship-caliber," teammate Greg Kelser said. "That made it just unbelievably exciting for us because when you're not a threat, you know your season's going to end and you know you're going to be sitting back watching other teams go for it all."

Kelser was a talented forward. He averaged 21.7 points and 10.8 rebounds per game as a sophomore in 1976–77. Vincent was a center who, like Johnson, grew up in Lansing. Those three players instantly turned the Spartans into winners. They started the season 15–1.

After a brief slump, Michigan State finished 23–4 with a 15–3 record in the Big Ten. They won their first Big Ten title since 1967, when they finished tied for first. Johnson was named the Big Ten Freshman of the Year. And the Spartans were headed to the National Collegiate Athletic Association (NCAA) Tournament for the first time in 19 years.

The Spartans quickly made an impact in the tournament. They cruised to an easy 77–63 win over Providence in the first round. Then came a 90–69 victory over Western Kentucky. Kelser and junior guard Robert Chapman each scored 23 points. Johnson added 14 assists.

Michigan State forward Greg Kelser
soars to the basket during the 1979
Final Four against Pennsylvania.

Michigan State's magical run came to an end in the Elite Eight against Kentucky. The game was tied 41–41 with less than seven minutes remaining. Then Kentucky's Kyle Macy scored and converted a free-throw attempt for a three-point play. He also hit six free throws in the final three minutes. That gave Kentucky a 52–49 win and ended the Spartans' season.

SPARTANS

ANOTHER STAR

Earvin "Magic" Johnson received more attention from the media during his career at Michigan State. But forward Greg Kelser was a solid all-around player as well. He could both score and rebound.

Kelser played for the Spartans from 1975 to 1979. He was the team's top scorer during his final three seasons at Michigan State, including the 1978–79 season, when he averaged 18.8 points. Kelser also led the Spartans in rebounding all four years he played for the school. His best season came in 1976–77, when he averaged 21.7 points and 10.8 rebounds per game.

Through 2011, Kelser remained Michigan State's all-time leading rebounder with 1,092 for his career. That ranked fifth all-time in Big Ten history through the 2010–11 season. His 2,014 career points ranked fourth in school history.

It was a heartbreaking end to the season for Michigan State. However, the team's 25 wins were the most in school history.

The 1977–78 season was only a preview of how good the Spartans could be. With Kelser, Johnson, and Vincent all returning, the Spartans were considered a favorite to win the national title the next season. In fact, they earned the number-one ranking in the nation after a mid-season win.

Remaining the top-ranked team would not be easy. The Spartans needed a big rally to overcome a 42–29 second-half deficit against Minnesota. Johnson had 12 assists and junior forward Ron Charles scored 19 points in a 69–62 win. Later, the Spartans went on the road to face Illinois. Both teams were undefeated at the time. After jumping out to an early 20–9 lead, Michigan State began to struggle. Illinois hit an 18-foot shot with three seconds left to hand the Spartans their first loss, 57–55.

[8]

Earvin "Magic" Johnson delivers a pass to a teammate during a 1979 NCAA Tournament game against Notre Dame.

The loss started a stretch of games in which Michigan State struggled. By the end of January, the Spartans were 4–4 in Big Ten play. They finally turned the season around with an overtime win over Ohio State. That started a 10-game winning streak. The Spartans finished with a 13–5 conference record and a share of the Big Ten title.

Michigan State fans were excited for the NCAA Tournament. The Spartans were playing their best basketball of the season when the tournament began. It had expanded from 32 teams to 40 teams that year. After a first-round bye, the Spartans rolled past three opponents to reach the Final Four for the first time since 1957.

The Spartans' national semifinal was never very close. Michigan State raced to a 38–8 lead over Pennsylvania. The lead grew to 50–17 at the half. The Spartans won the game 101–67. Kelser had 28 points and nine

[9]

Earvin "Magic" Johnson cuts down the nets after Michigan State beat Indiana State for the 1979 NCAA title.

rebounds. But Johnson was the biggest star. He had a triple-double with 29 points, 10 rebounds, and 10 assists.

The win set up the showdown that many fans had been waiting for. The top-ranked Indiana State Sycamores had a star forward named Larry Bird. Like Johnson, he was one of the best players in the country. Both could score, rebound, and pass as well as anybody. And both had led their teams to success that season. Bird's Sycamores had 33 wins and no losses going into the championship game. Michigan State was 25–6 and ranked third.

A record number of fans tuned in to watch the game on television. They saw the Spartans take control early. Once again, they were never really threatened.

Bird struggled against Michigan State's zone defense. He made only seven of his 21 shots and scored 19 points. He grabbed 13 rebounds but had six turnovers. And he had only two assists.

Despite Bird's struggles, Indiana State was trailing by only seven points with six minutes remaining. The Spartans ran a minute off the clock—there was no shot clock at the time—before Kelser found Johnson cutting to the basket. He made a perfect pass and Johnson went up for a dunk. That bumped the Spartans' lead to nine. On the play, Bob Heaton was called for a flagrant foul. That gave Johnson two free throws as well. Johnson calmly hit both shots to give Michigan State a 61–50 lead with 5:05 left. The lead was too much for Indiana State to overcome, and the Spartans earned a 75–64 victory.

Johnson scored 24 points, grabbed seven rebounds, and had five assists. Kelser added 19 points. Guard Terry Donnelly, who had averaged only 6.3 points per game that season, added 15 points.

It was the basketball program's first national title. It would not be the last.

JAY VINCENT

When Greg Kelser and Earvin "Magic" Johnson left Michigan State after the 1978–79 season, forward/center Jay Vincent proved how talented he was. Vincent led the team in scoring in 1979–80 with an average of 21.6 points per game. The next season he again led the Spartans in scoring, averaging 22.6 points. He also led the team with 8.5 rebounds per game.

Michigan State was originally known as
State Agricultural College.

BABY STEPS

MICHIGAN STATE UNIVERSITY BASKETBALL WAS BORN IN THE MIDDLE OF THE WINTER IN 1899. THE FIRST GAME THE SCHOOL PLAYED WAS AGAINST OLIVET ON FEBRUARY 27. OLIVET WON THE GAME 7–6. TWO WEEKS LATER, THE SAME SCHOOLS FACED EACH OTHER AGAIN. AGAIN, OLIVET WON. THIS TIME THE SCORE WAS 15–6.

The program has changed a lot since those first two games. For one, the school was then known as State Agricultural College. Also, the school's nickname was not yet the Spartans. The team was originally called the Aggies. In the early years, though, one part of the program was similar to the modern Spartans: the team won a lot of games.

Michigan State played only 14 games from the 1900–01 season through the 1902–03 season. Yet they won all 14 of them. Chester L. Brewer took over as Michigan State's third head coach in 1904. The team went 70–25 under Brewer and never had a losing season during his seven years there.

One of Brewer's biggest accomplishments came on January 9, 1909. Michigan State traveled to Ann Arbor to face the Michigan Wolverines for the first time. The Wolverines are still the Spartans' biggest rival. Michigan State won the first game between the two schools, 24–16. Just over a month later, the Spartans won a rematch in East Lansing, 45–23.

Five different coaches guided the Michigan State program from 1911 through the end of the 1925–26 season. Benjamin VanAlstyne took over in 1926. He was the coach for 22 years—the longest time of any coach in the program's history through 2011. His 17 winning seasons also remained a school record.

Assistant coach Alton Kircher took over after VanAlstyne retired. He lasted just one season before Pete Newell took over in 1950. That season also marked Michigan State's first as a member of the Big Ten Conference. Michigan State won its first Big Ten game on January 6, 1951, defeating the Northwestern Wildcats 67–62. Under Newell, the Spartans were a successful team. However, it was not until Forrest "Forddy" Anderson took over in 1954 that they took the next step.

THE CHESTER L. BREWER AWARD

Michigan State gives out the Chester L. Brewer Award each year to a graduating senior for his or her outstanding performance in both athletics and academics and "for possessing a high degree of character, personality, competitive spirit, and other leadership qualities which forecast a successful future."

Anderson's leadership and talented players such as forward Julius McCoy, center Johnny Green, and forward/guard Jack Quiggle led the Spartans to a new level of success. In 1955–56, McCoy scored a school-record 600 points and averaged 27.2 points per game. He also led the team in rebounding, averaging 10 per game.

The 1956–57 season was one of firsts for the Spartans. The school won a share of its first Big Ten title, finishing 10–4. After the Spartans lost their first three conference games, Green and Quiggle led the team to 10 straight wins. Quiggle scored 15.3 points per game to lead the team

BABY STEPS

and also averaged 5.6 rebounds. In his first season with the Spartans, Green chipped in an average 13.2 points and a team-leading 14.6 rebounds per game.

The NCAA Tournament began in 1939. However, early tournaments were much smaller than today's version. As conference champions, Michigan State played in the tournament for the first time in 1956–57. The Spartans made it a memorable debut. After beating Notre Dame in the first round, Michigan State faced powerful Kentucky. The Spartans pulled off the upset. They beat the Wildcats 80–68 to advance to the Final Four in Kansas City, Missouri.

The North Carolina Tar Heels awaited in the national semifinals. The game turned into a classic. Michigan State held a two-point lead with 11 seconds remaining in the first overtime period. Green had a chance to win the game at the free-throw line. All he had to do was make the first shot. There was no three-point line at the time.

So if Green had made a free throw, North Carolina would have needed to score twice. But Green missed. Pete Brennan of North Carolina grabbed the rebound. He then quickly dribbled down the court. Right before the buzzer sounded he took a shot. The ball went through the hoop to tie the game and force a second overtime. Finally, after three overtime periods, North Carolina came out the winner, 74–70.

The Spartans won the conference title again in 1959. That got them into the NCAA Tournament for the second time. However, Michigan State lost to Louisville 88–81 in the second round.

Quiggle and Green graduated after that. The Spartans struggled for the next six seasons. They experienced only one winning season during that time. Michigan State bottomed out in 1964–65. It finished 1–13 in conference play and 5–18 overall. It was Anderson's last season as the Spartans' coach.

John Benington took over in 1965. He guided Michigan State to a second-place finish in the Big Ten. The Spartans then tied Indiana for the Big Ten title in 1967. There was no playoff to determine the

JOHNNY BE GOOD

Center Johnny Green was a key member of the Michigan State team that advanced to the Final Four in 1957 and the NCAA Tournament in 1959. After averaging 13.2 points and 14.6 rebounds in 1956–57, he scored 18 points per game and averaged a school single-season-record 17.8 rebounds the next season. As a senior in 1958–59, he averaged 18.5 points and 16.6 rebounds per game.

BABY STEPS

Coach Jud Heathcote helped turn around Michigan State's fortunes when he arrived in 1976.

conference champion. According to a conference rule at that time, the NCAA Tournament bid went to the team that had been absent from the tournament longer. Thus, Indiana advanced instead of the Spartans.

Benington coached Michigan State for two more seasons before Gus Ganakas took over in 1969. Ganakas went 89–84 during his seven

HIGH SCORERS

While most people think today's college basketball teams are high scoring, Michigan State's two highest- scoring teams played in the 1960s. The 1963–64 squad holds the school record with 92.1 points per game. The next season the Spartans averaged 85.9 points, the second-highest average in team history through 2010–11.

seasons at Michigan State. But the program was unable to achieve the same success it had under Anderson or Benington. The Spartans' best finish in Big Ten play was a fourth-place showing in 1973–74.

Things finally began to change in 1976, when Jud Heathcote was hired as the school's 15th head coach. Michigan State would soon become a basketball power.

Michigan State's Earvin "Magic" Johnson pushes away a no-look pass during a 1978 game against Illinois.

THE HEATHCOTE ERA

JUD HEATHCOTE CAME TO MICHIGAN STATE FROM THE UNIVERSITY OF MONTANA IN 1976. AT MONTANA, HE WAS 80–53 AND WON TWO BIG SKY CONFERENCE CHAMPIONSHIPS. IT DID NOT TAKE HIM LONG TO TURN AROUND A MICHIGAN STATE PROGRAM THAT HAD BECOME AVERAGE.

The Spartans experienced 13 winning seasons during Heathcote's 19 years in charge. After a 12–15 record in his first season, Michigan State improved to 25–5 in 1977–78. That gave the team its fourth Big Ten title. Behind point guard Earvin "Magic" Johnson, forward Greg Kelser, and forward/center Jay Vincent, the Spartans then came within one game of the Final Four.

Then came the magical 1979 national title. Johnson received most of the attention during his time at Michigan State. But two talented players in Kelser and Vincent provided plenty of help.

AGONY OF DEFEAT

Jud Heathcote and the Spartans experienced the joy of victory by winning the national title in 1979, but they also experienced the agony of defeat several times during his coaching tenure. In the 1986 NCAA Tournament, Michigan State faced the Kansas Jayhawks in the Sweet 16. During the second half, the clock accidentally stopped running for about 15 seconds. That extra time allowed Kansas to tie the game in regulation. The Jayhawks then pulled away for a 96–86 overtime win.

In the 1990 Sweet 16, the Georgia Tech Yellow Jackets beat the Spartans 81–80 in overtime. However, the game should have never gone to an extra period. Kenny Anderson of Georgia Tech sank a shot at the end of regulation to tie the game. However, the shot should not have counted. Replays showed the shot came after time had run out.

Kelser led the team in scoring and rebounding in 1978–79. He averaged 18.8 points and 8.7 rebounds per game. For his career he averaged 17.5 points and 9.5 rebounds per game. Through 2011, he was the only Michigan State player to score more than 2,000 points and grab more than 1,000 rebounds in a career.

Both Johnson and Kelser left after the 1979 season to join the National Basketball Association (NBA). Vincent stayed at Michigan State through 1981. He scored 1,914 points during his career. He led the team in scoring in both 1979–80 and 1980–81 and was named the Big Ten Player of the Year in 1981. However, the Spartans reached the postseason only once in the five years after their national title. That was in 1983, when they played in the National Invitation Tournament (NIT).

Michigan State made back-to-back NCAA Tournament appearances in 1985 and 1986. Guards Sam Vincent—the brother of Jay Vincent—and Scott Skiles were the stars of those teams. Sam Vincent led the 1984–85 team by averaging 23 points, four assists, and 3.9 rebounds per game.

Skiles played for the Spartans from 1982 to 1986. The point guard was outstanding during his senior season. He averaged 27.4 points, 6.5 assists, and 4.4 rebounds per game. He led the Big Ten in scoring with 29.1 points per game during conference play. He also led the Spartans in assists per game during each of his four seasons. However, the Spartans lost in the NCAA Tournament's first round in 1985 and in the Sweet 16 in 1986.

The Spartans returned to the postseason in 1988–89. Despite going 6–12 in Big Ten play, they finished the regular season 15–13 to earn an invitation to the NIT. Michigan State won three games in the NIT before losing in the semifinals.

Guard Steve Smith was the standout player for the Spartans from 1987 to 1991. He led the team in scoring three times. As a sophomore in 1988–89, he led the team in both scoring and rebounding with 17.7 points and 6.9 rebounds per game. He increased his scoring to 20.2 points per game the next season. As a senior in 1990–91, he scored 25.1 points per game and grabbed 6.1 rebounds.

Smith graduated in 1991. But Heathcote recruited talented guard Shawn Respert to replace him. Respert was known for his great shooting ability. However, he suffered an injury that limited him to only one game in the 1990–91 season. College athletes are only allowed to compete for four seasons. However, an exception was made for Respert and he was able to star for the team over the next four seasons. He left the program as the all-time leading scorer with 2,531 points.

TOUGH LOVE

Jud Heathcote was known as a tough coach to play for. How tough was he? One of his star players nearly quit in 1990. "Coach can make you or break you," guard Shawn Respert said. "He almost broke me, I admit it. How close was I to leaving? Well, my mother talked me out of it. Otherwise, I don't know. But I came to realize the only thing Jud wanted was for me to be a better player. I am where I am today because of him."

Michigan State guard Steve Smith
dribbles down the court during a
1990 game.

With Smith and then Respert leading the way, the Spartans were
now a basketball power. They did not win a national title, but Michigan
State made seven straight postseason appearances from 1988–89 to
1994–95. In 1989–90, the Spartans won the Big Ten title with a 15–3
record.

Shawn Respert averaged 25.6 points per game during his senior season. He left as the Spartans' all-time leading scorer.

Michigan State finished second in the Big Ten in 1994–95, going 14–4. The Spartans entered the NCAA Tournament with a 22–5 record and a number-three seed. But they were stunned in the first round. The Weber State Wildcats beat them 79–72. Heathcote retired after that season.

HE SAID IT

"Magic [Johnson] was the greatest player I ever coached by a long ways. We had a lot of great guards, Sam Vincent, Scott Skiles, etc. We don't compare these players to Magic. Magic was the coach on and off the floor. He wanted to win. He was not selfish. He and I were always on the same page. He's a great player and personality." —former Michigan State head coach Jud Heathcote

In 19 seasons as the team's head coach, Heathcote compiled a 340–220 record. He guided the Spartans to three Big Ten titles and one national title. He turned Michigan State into a perennial winner and regular NCAA Tournament participant. The Spartans appeared in the NCAA Tournament nine times under Heathcote and made three trips to the NIT as well.

Upon Heathcote's retirement, the reins of the program were handed to assistant coach Tom Izzo. The move turned out to be a good one.

Michigan State guard Mateen Cleaves pushes the ball up the court during the 2000 NCAA Final Four.

4

CHAMPIONS AGAIN

TOM IZZO SERVED AS AN ASSISTANT COACH UNDER JUD HEATHCOTE FOR MORE THAN 10 YEARS. WHEN HEATHCOTE RETIRED IN 1995, HE HAND-PICKED IZZO TO BECOME HEAD COACH. IZZO QUICKLY SHOWED HE WAS READY TO LEAD MICHIGAN STATE.

The Spartans made back-to-back appearances in the NIT during Izzo's first two seasons. The coach was also bringing in talented players. Izzo convinced forward Morris Peterson, guard Mateen Cleaves, guard Charlie Bell, and forward Andre Hutson to become Spartans.

Peterson came to Michigan State in 1995, but he appeared in only four games that season because of an injury. By the time he graduated after the 1999–2000 season, he had scored 1,588 points. He averaged 11.6 points and 4.7 rebounds per game. Peterson became a full-time starter in 1999–2000.

SPARTANS

Cleaves came to Michigan State in 1996 and was a starter from the beginning. He averaged 10.2 points and five assists per game as a freshman. In 1997–98 he averaged 16.1 points and 7.2 assists per game. By the end of his career, Cleaves had scored 1,541 points and was a three-time All-American. He also led the Spartans in assists in each of his four seasons. He finished his career with 816.

Bell and Hutson each played from 1997 to 2001. Bell averaged 10.5 points per game and 4.5 rebounds for the Spartans during his career. Hutson averaged 10.1 points and 6.1 rebounds per game during his career. Twice he led the team in rebounding.

Peterson, Cleaves, Bell, and Hutson helped the Spartans reach new heights. In 1998–99, Michigan State lost to Wisconsin in the first conference game of the season. Then the Spartans rolled off 22 straight wins. They claimed the conference title, the Big Ten Tournament title, and advanced to the Final Four for the first time since 1979.

In the national semifinals, Michigan State faced Duke. Both teams entered the tournament as number-one seeds. Everyone was hoping

WHAT A STREAK

Helping the Spartans reach the Final Four in 1999 was an incredible 22-game win streak. The streak started on January 9, 1999, when Michigan State defeated Michigan 81–67. The Spartans did not lose again until March 27, when Duke earned a 68–62 win in the national semifinals. The previous school record for the longest winning streak was 16 games, set twice.

[30]

to see a good game. And they got one. Duke led 32–30 at halftime. But Michigan State struggled shooting in the second half. When the final buzzer sounded, Duke claimed a 68–62 win. Michigan State ended the season with a team-record 33 wins.

The loss to Duke was a difficult way to end the season. But the Spartans got some good news after the season. Cleaves decided to remain at Michigan State for his senior season rather than enter the NBA Draft. With his return, as well as the return of Peterson, Hutson, and Bell, the Spartans were considered a contender for the national title in 1999–2000.

CHAMPIONS AGAIN

THE UNSUNG HERO

Seniors Morris Peterson and Mateen Cleaves received most of the attention during the Spartans' 1999–2000 season. Senior A. J. Granger had several big moments as well. But he saved his best for last. In the national title game against Florida, Granger matched his career high with 19 points to help carry the Spartans to victory. One of Granger's strengths was his three-point shooting. He made three of five against Florida.

"We called him the 'X' factor going into the game," Florida coach Billy Donovan said. "We knew that Mateen Cleaves and Morris Peterson were going to probably play well and do a good job handling our press."

Said Granger: "I'm not the go-to guy, so I got more good shots. They [Cleaves and Peterson] got me open tonight, set some picks for me. Then, I just had to make the shots. It just seems like somebody on this team steps up every night."

The team did not disappoint. The Spartans rolled through the regular season with a 23–7 record. They claimed a share of the Big Ten regular-season title by going 13–3. Then they won the Big Ten Tournament, defeating their three opponents by an average of 11.3 points.

Michigan State again entered the NCAA Tournament as a top seed. The Spartans opened with a 65–38 win over Valparaiso. Then came three more wins by an average of 13.3 points. No team could stop the Spartans. The trend continued in the Final Four in Indianapolis, Indiana.

In the national semifinals, Michigan State took on Big Ten rival Wisconsin. It was the fourth meeting of the season between the two schools. The Spartans had won the first three games. They won the fourth showdown as well, 53–41. Peterson poured in 20 points, Cleaves scored 11, and Hutson added 10 points and 10 rebounds.

The Spartans faced Florida in the national championship game. The Gators were expected to give the Spartans a tough game. But Michigan State controlled the game from start to finish, despite receiving a scare in the second half. Cleaves missed several minutes with an ankle sprain. But Michigan State's depth was too much for Florida to handle as the Spartans won 89–76. Peterson scored 21 points to lead the team. Senior forward A. J. Granger added 19 points and nine rebounds. Cleaves had 18 points and four assists and Bell had nine points and eight rebounds.

For the first time since 1979, the Spartans were national champions. It was only Izzo's fifth season as head coach, and he had guided Michigan State to the top of college basketball. Over the next decade, he would keep the Spartans there.

[33]

CHAMPIONS AGAIN

Michigan State guard Jason Richardson dunks against Iowa during a 2001 game.

STAYING ELITE

MATEEN CLEAVES AND MORRIS PETERSON GRADUATED AFTER THE 2000 NATIONAL TITLE SEASON AND WENT TO THE NBA. SOME FANS FEARED THE TEAM WOULD SUFFER A LETDOWN WITHOUT THEIR TWO STARS. BUT THE SPARTANS CONTINUED TO WIN, NOT JUST IN 2000–01, BUT FOR THE NEXT DECADE.

The Spartans began the 2000–01 season with 12 straight wins. Leading the way were seniors Charlie Bell and Andre Hutson and sophomore guard Jason Richardson. Bell averaged 13.5 points, a team-leading 5.1 assists, and 4.7 rebounds during his senior season. Hutson added 13.8 points and led the team with 7.6 rebounds per game. Richardson led the team in scoring, averaging 14.7 points per game.

The Spartans claimed a share of the 2001 Big Ten title and again entered the NCAA Tournament as a number-one seed. Michigan State advanced to the Sweet 16 for the fourth straight season. The Spartans then defeated Gonzaga and

SPARTANS

COACH IZZO

On November 29, 2009, Tom Izzo set the Michigan State record for victories with a 106–68 win over the Massachusetts Minutemen. The win was Izzo's 341st at Michigan State, surpassing Jud Heathcote. After the win, Spartan players doused Izzo with water.

"I guess in some ways I'm happy that they appreciate even I want to leave some footprint here somewhere," Izzo said after the game. "Maybe that's what meant as much as anything. I think they were genuinely excited about it and I hope they feel a part of it."

Izzo was an assistant coach under Heathcote for more than a decade and was hand-picked by Heathcote to take over the Michigan State program after his retirement. "Jud had been so instrumental on my behalf and got me the job, that I'll just look at it as we have 681 wins between us," Izzo said. "We'll count that as a record."

Temple to reach the Final Four for the third straight year.

Only the Arizona Wildcats stood in the way of a return trip to the national championship game. The game was close at the half. Arizona led 32–30. But the Wildcats pulled away in the second half for an 80–61 victory. In their last game as Spartans, Hutson scored 20 points while Bell grabbed 10 rebounds.

Michigan State advanced to the NCAA Tournament again from 2002 to 2004. But the Spartans were unable to return to the Final Four. During this stretch, guard Chris Hill was the top player. He led the team in scoring with 13.7 points per game as a sophomore in 2002–03.

Michigan State returned to the Final Four in 2005 thanks to the play of guard Maurice Ager, center Paul Davis, and Hill. Ager led the team with 14.1 points per game. Davis grabbed eight rebounds per game. Hill led the team in assists with 4.3 per game.

The 2005 Spartans were not as dominant as their previous Final Four teams were. They finished second in the Big Ten with a 13–3 record and lost in the first round of the Big Ten Tournament. The team entered the NCAA Tournament as a number-five seed. However, it picked up momentum there. After winning its first two games, Michigan State upset Duke 78–68 in the Sweet 16. Then their Elite Eight game against Kentucky became a classic.

Patrick Sparks of Kentucky hit a three-pointer at the end of regulation to force overtime. The teams remained tied after one overtime period and had to play a second. The Spartans scored the first five points and pulled away to win 94–88. Guard Shannon Brown was the player of the game for Michigan State, scoring 24 points.

North Carolina was up next in the national semifinals. The Tar Heels had come into the tournament as a number-one seed. But Michigan State appeared ready to pull off the upset.

The Spartans led 38–33 at the half. Then North Carolina rallied. With the game tied at 49, the Tar Heels scored 12 straight points to take control. North Carolina won 87–71.

Michigan State reached the NCAA Tournament in each of the next three seasons. But the Spartans did not advance past the Sweet 16. The team had extra motivation to get back to the Final Four in 2009. It would be held in nearby Detroit, Michigan, that year.

The 2009 Spartans had another outstanding team. They won the Big Ten regular-season title with a 15–3 record and entered the NCAA Tournament as a number-two seed. After winning its first two games, Michigan State overcame a 13-point deficit to beat Kansas 67–62. The win set up a showdown against Louisville in the Elite Eight. The Cardinals were the tournament's overall number-one seed. The Spartans held a one-point lead in the second half. But then Michigan State went on a 21–7 run to pull out a 64–52 win. Center Goran Suton led the Spartans with 19 points and 10 rebounds.

Playing in Detroit and in front of a host of hometown fans, the Spartans faced Connecticut. The Huskies were another number-one

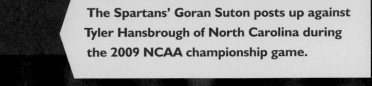

The Spartans' Goran Suton posts up against Tyler Hansbrough of North Carolina during the 2009 NCAA championship game.

seed. But they were no match for the Spartans, who won 82–73. Guard Kalin Lucas led Michigan State with 21 points. The Spartans then faced North Carolina in the national championship game. The Tar Heels were the third number-one seed in a row for the Spartans.

This time, however, Michigan State could not match up. The Tar Heels built a 55–34 lead at the half and went on to win 89–72. In the first half, the Tar Heels made nearly 53 percent of their shots. Meanwhile, Michigan State had 14 first-half turnovers.

STAYING ELITE

Michigan State's Kalin Lucas brings the ball up the court during the 2011 NCAA Tournament.

"That first five minutes of the game, we couldn't stop it," Spartans guard Travis Walton said. "When we did try to stop it, we had good looks, we didn't make the shots. And they kept pushing and pushing at us. They were getting to the free-throw line and we were turning the ball over."

The Spartans were back in the Final Four again in 2010. But they were facing a team that was the story of the tournament—the Butler Bulldogs. Butler is a smaller school located in Indianapolis, Indiana. That was also the city where the Final Four was being held. Many people wanted to see Butler win and continue its tournament run. Michigan State kept the game close. Guard Durrell Summers scored 14 points and grabbed 10 rebounds. But the Bulldogs held on to win 52–50.

The 2010–11 season did not go as planned for the Spartans. The team struggled all year and finished 19–15. Still, the team made the NCAA Tournament for the 14th straight season. But the Spartans lost to the University of California, Los Angeles Bruins in the first round.

The loss brought an end to a tough season. But with Izzo at the helm, fans could have faith that the Spartans would be back in the Final Four again soon.

END OF A FINE CAREER

Kalin Lucas's career at Michigan State ended after the 2010–11 season. The guard had an outstanding career for the Spartans. He left as the school's fifth all-time leading scorer with 1,996 points. Lucas left as the all-time leader in free throws made with 507 and free-throw attempts with 637. His 558 assists ranked sixth in school history. Lucas was also a three-time All-Big Ten honoree and was the 2009 Big Ten Player of the Year.

TIMELINE

State Agricultural College plays its first basketball game on February 27. The team loses 7–6 to Olivet.

Michigan State begins a streak in which it does not lose a single game in three seasons, winning 14 straight games before losing its first game of the 1904 season.

Chester L. Brewer becomes head coach. He leads the team until 1910 and goes 70–25 during his tenure.

Benjamin VanAlstyne takes over the program. He coaches the Spartans for 22 years before retiring in 1949. During his 22 years as coach, he wins 231 games, the third-most in school history through 2011.

Michigan State defeats Indiana 76–61 to claim a share of the Big Ten Conference title, the school's first.

1899 1901 1904 1926 1957

In the national championship game, Johnson leads the Spartans to their first title with a 75–64 win over Larry Bird and Indiana State on March 26.

On March 17, Michigan State loses to the Weber State Wildcats 79–72 in the opening round of the NCAA Tournament. The loss brings an end to the coaching career of Heathcote.

Assistant coach Tom Izzo is hand-picked by Heathcote to become the new head coach of the Spartans.

The Spartans return to the NCAA Tournament for the first time since 1995 and win their first Big Ten title since 1990. Michigan State loses to North Carolina in the Sweet 16.

Michigan State returns to the Final Four for the first time since winning the national championship in 1979.

1979 1995 1995 1998 1999

The Spartans qualify for the NCAA Tournament for the first time and reach the Final Four, but they lose to North Carolina in triple overtime in the national semifinals.

For the second time in three years, the Spartans win the Big Ten title and qualify for the NCAA Tournament. Michigan State loses to the Louisville Cardinals in the second round.

Jud Heathcote becomes the head coach of Michigan State. Heathcote would coach for 19 years. He left with 340 career wins, the most in school history at the time.

Michigan State wins the Big Ten title with a 15–3 conference record. It advances to the regional semifinals before losing to the Kentucky Wildcats 52–49 on March 18.

On March 24, Earvin "Magic" Johnson records his eighth triple-double of the season against Pennsylvania in the national semifinal.

1957 | 1959 | 1976 | 1978 | 1979

A school-record 22-game winning streak comes to an end on March 27 when the Spartans lose to the Duke Blue Devils 68–62 in the national semifinals.

The Spartans win their second national title, beating the Florida Gators 89–76 on April 3. Michigan State won its final 11 games of the season en route to winning the title.

Michigan State returns to the Final Four for the third straight year but loses to Arizona in the national semifinals.

On April 6, Michigan State loses to North Carolina in the national championship game in front of a record-setting crowd in Detroit, Michigan.

Michigan State reaches the Final Four for the second straight season. The Spartans lose in the national semifinals to the Butler Bulldogs, 52–50.

1999 | 2000 | 2001 | 2009 | 2010

QUICK STATS

PROGRAM INFO

State Agricultural College Aggies
   (1899–1908)
Michigan Agricultural College Aggies
   (1909–24)
Michigan State College of Agriculture and
   Applied Science Spartans (1925–54)
Michigan State University of Agriculture
   and Applied Science Spartans
   (1955–63)
Michigan State University Spartans
   (1964–)

NCAA FINALS
(WINS IN BOLD)
1979, **2000**, 2009

OTHER ACHIEVEMENTS
Final Fours: 8
NCAA Tournaments: 25
Big Ten Tournament titles: 2

KEY PLAYERS
(POSITION(S); YEARS WITH TEAM)
Mateen Cleaves (G; 1996–2000)
Johnny Green (C; 1956–59)
Earvin "Magic" Johnson (G; 1977–79)

* All statistics through 2010–11 season

Greg Kelser (F; 1975–79)
Kalin Lucas (G; 2007–11)
Julius McCoy (F; 1953–56)
Morris Peterson (F; 1995–2000)
Shawn Respert (G;1990–95)
Scott Skiles (G; 1982–86)
Steve Smith (G; 1987–91)
Jay Vincent (C/F; 1977–81)
Sam Vincent (G; 1981–85)

KEY COACHES
Jud Heathcote (1976–95):
   340–220; 14–8 (NCAA Tournament)
Tom Izzo (1996–):
   383–161; 35–13 (NCAA
   Tournament)

HOME ARENA
Breslin Center (1989–)

"I'm crushed and disappointed because we just got off to such a poor start, and yet I'm so proud of these guys. They've been knocked down so many times this year that I don't think I've ever had a team that's gone through as much, and yet to battle back and almost put themselves at a chance to win was incredible. . . . I give UCLA a lot of credit. They just seemed to have more energy than us early. We found a way to bounce back . . . and we just fell a little short." —Michigan State coach Tom Izzo after losing in the first round of the 2011 NCAA Tournament to the University of California, Los Angeles Bruins

"We are the blue-collar team. This is the blue-collar city. It was just amazing, amazing to walk out of that tunnel. . . . Yes, there were a lot of Michigan State fans in there. I think other people thought it was an incredible setting. I am appreciative for that. I'm appreciative for the people. I hope we were a ray of sunshine, a distraction for them, diversion, anything else we can be." —Michigan State coach Tom Izzo talking about playing in front of a record-breaking crowd at the 2009 Final Four in Detroit, Michigan

Michigan State has had many great players during its long history. But only one player has ever scored 50 points in a game. Terry Furlow poured in 50 points on January 5, 1976, against Iowa. Amazingly, Furlow almost reached 50 points again three days later. On January 8, he scored 48 points against Northwestern.

GLOSSARY

All-American
A player chosen as one of the best amateurs in the country in a particular activity.

assist
A pass that leads directly to a made shot.

conference
In sports, a group of teams that plays each other each season.

draft
A system used by professional sports leagues to select new players in order to spread incoming talent among all teams. The NBA Draft is held each June.

overtime
A period in a basketball game that is played to determine a winner when the four quarters end in a tie.

postseason
The tournaments scheduled for after the regular season and conference tournament, including the NCAA Tournament and the NIT.

rebound
To secure the basketball after a missed shot.

recruited
Attempted to entice a player to come to a certain school.

retired
Having officially ended one's career.

rival
An opponent that brings out great emotion in a team, its fans, and its players.

seed
In basketball, a ranking system used for tournaments. The best teams earn a number-one seed.

upset
A result where the supposedly worse team defeats the supposedly better team.

FOR MORE INFORMATION

FURTHER READING

Davis, Seth. *When March Went Mad: The Game That Transformed Basketball.* New York: Holt Paperbacks, 2010.

Ebling, Jack, and John Lewandowski. *Green Glory: Champions of the Hardwood.* Southfield, MI: Gametime Sports and Entertainment, 2001.

Kelser, Greg, and Steve Grinczel. *Gregory Kelser's Tales from Michigan State Basketball.* Champaign, IL: Sports Publishing, 2006.

WEB LINKS

To learn more about the Michigan State Spartans, visit ABDO Publishing Company online at **www.abdopublishing.com**. Web sites about the Spartans are featured on our Books Links page. These links are routinely monitored and updated to provide the most current information available.

PLACES TO VISIT

Breslin Student Events Center
One Birch Road
East Lansing, MI 48824
517-432-1989
www.breslincenter.com

This has been the Spartans' home arena since 1989. The arena is named after Jack Breslin, a Battle Creek, Michigan, native, who served his alma mater, Michigan State University, as a distinguished student leader, honored athlete, top administrator, and relentless advocate. Free tours are available by calling in advance.

College Basketball Experience
1401 Grand Boulevard
Kansas City, MO 64106
816-949-7500
www.collegebasketballexperience.com

This interactive museum allows visitors to experience various aspects of college basketball. It also includes the National Collegiate Basketball Hall of Fame, which highlights the greatest players, coaches, and moments in the history of college basketball. Earvin "Magic" Johnson and Jud Heathcote are among the former Spartans enshrined here.

INDEX

Ager, Maurice, 36

Anderson, Forrest "Forddy" (coach), 14–15, 17, 19

Bell, Charlie, 29–31, 33, 35–36

Benington, John (coach), 16, 17–18

Brewer, Chester L. (coach), 13–14

Brown, Shannon, 38

Chapman, Robert, 6

Charles, Ron, 8

Cleaves, Mateen, 29–33, 35

Davis, Paul, 36

Donnelly, Terry, 11

Ganakas, Gus, 18–19

Granger, A. J., 32, 33

Green, Johnny, 15–17

Heathcote, Jud (coach), 19, 21, 22, 24, 26–27, 29, 36

Hill, Chris, 36

Hutson, Andre, 29–32, 35–36

Izzo, Tom (coach), 5, 27, 29, 33, 36, 41

Johnson, Earvin "Magic," 5–6, 8, 10–11, 21–22, 27

Kelser, Greg, 5–6, 8–9, 11, 21–22

Kircher, Alton (coach), 14

Lucas, Kalin, 39, 41

McCoy, Julius, 15, 16

NCAA Tournament finals
1979, 10–11, 21
2000, 33
2009, 39–40

Newell, Pete (coach), 14

NIT, 22, 24, 27, 29

Peterson, Morris, 29–33, 35

Quiggle, Jack, 15–16, 17

Respert, Shawn, 24–25

Richardson, Jason, 35

Skiles, Scott, 23, 27

Smith, Steve, 24–25

Summers, Durrell, 41

Suton, Goran, 38

VanAlstyne, Benjamin (coach), 14

Vincent, Jay, 5–6, 8, 11, 21, 23

Vincent, Sam, 22, 23, 27

Walton, Travis, 40

ABOUT THE AUTHOR

J Chris Roselius is a freelance writer based in Houston, Texas. A graduate of the University of Texas, he has written more than a dozen books on a variety of topics. He has won several awards for feature and column writing from the Associated Press during his career. Roselius enjoys spending his spare time with his wife and coaching his two children in Little League baseball.